Pins in
the Map

by Nancy Day

illustrated by George Hamblin

Editorial Offices: Glenview, Illinois • Parsippany, New Jersey • New York, New York
Sales Offices: Needham, Massachusetts • Duluth, Georgia • Glenview, Illinois
Coppell, Texas • Ontario, California • Mesa, Arizona

Photographs

Every effort has been made to secure permission and provide appropriate credit for photographic material. The publisher deeply regrets any omission and pledges to correct errors called to its attention in subsequent editions.

Unless otherwise acknowledged, all photographs are the property of Pearson Education, Inc.

Photo locators denoted as follows: Top (T), Center (C), Bottom (B), Left (L), Right (R), Background (Bkgd)

16 Darren Baker/Fotolia

Illustrations George Hamblin.

ISBN: 0-328-13186-5

"Here, Boots," Katie called outside her family's cottage. Her cat didn't come to her.

"I hope he's not in the motel," Katie thought to herself. She went into the motel's lobby.

Boots was sitting on a boy's lap.

"Boots!" Katie scolded. "You're not supposed to bother guests."

"I'm Sam," the boy smiled. "Boots isn't bothering me at all. He looks like my cat at home—wherever that is." Sam's mouth turned down.

"I'm Katie. Are you visiting? Where do you live?" Katie asked.

"I live here at your motel until my parents find a house," Sam replied. "My mom will be working here in Grand Haven, so we have to relocate. We used to live in Santa Fe, New Mexico."

"I know about relocating. I have moved from one location to another my whole life," Katie said, pointing to a big map of the United States on the wall. "I've put pins in the spots where I've lived. Our motel guests stick in pins too."

Sam placed a pin in Santa Fe.

"First, we lived in New York City,"
Katie pointed. "We lived in a tiny
apartment in a really tall building."

"What do you remember most about
living there?" asked Sam.

"My dad worked in a big hotel. I remember watching people going in and out of the spinning door when I visited him at work. It was fun to watch all the people!" Katie laughed. "Then Dad got a job with a different hotel."

"Where did you move then?"
Sam asked.

"All the way across the country to
Pacifica, California." Katie showed him
the pin. "It's near San Francisco. We
packed our car. We drove for five days.
My brother was too young to play any
games with me. He cried all the way!"

"It was great when we got there," Katie went on. "I could see the ocean from my bedroom window!"

"It was nice," Katie said. "The only trouble was that our house was the same shape as every other house! I could tell which one was ours only by the color and the gnome in the front yard."

"Next, we moved to Branchville, South Carolina," said Katie. "My parents ran a peach farm there. It wasn't so bad taking the long route to get there. My brother could play games by that time!" Katie chuckled.

Sam asked, "What did you do in Branchville?"

"I spent days watching my parents work on the old farmhouse. Sometimes I helped sell peaches at our stand. I'll never forget the smell of ripe peaches, and how the juice runs down your chin when you eat one," Katie smiled.

"So you moved again," Sam said.
"Yes," Katie answered. "My parents sold the farm and bought this motel. It wasn't such a long car trip to get here. And here I get to see Lake Michigan."

13

"Do you like living in this town?" Sam asked, his voice a little unsure.

"I do!" said Katie. "I like it more than anywhere else. Everybody knows everybody else. People are nice and friendly."

"Like you," Sam said.

Katie smiled. "It's fun meeting new people at the motel."

"I didn't want to move away from my friends and the mountains," Sam said. "But now I think I'm going to like living here." Sam pulled his pin out of Santa Fe and handed it to Katie.

Katie stuck the pin into Grand Haven.

On the Move

Millions of Americans move each year. There are almost as many reasons to relocate as there are people who move! Sometimes people relocate for better jobs. Some move to be closer to family members. Others want to live in a different kind of place. It can be exciting to move to a new place!